MISSION SURVIVAL:
SAVING EARTH'S ENDANGERED ANIMALS

SAVING THE GORILLA

LOUISE SPILSBURY

CHERITON
CHILDREN'S BOOKS

Published in 2023 by **Cheriton Children's Books**
PO Box 7258, Bridgnorth WV16 9ET, UK

First Edition

Author: Louise Spilsbury
Designer: Paul Myerscough
Editor: Jane Brooke
Proofreader: Tracey Kelly
Consultant: David Hawksett, BSc

Picture credits: Cover: Shutterstock/Sam Chadwick. Inside: p1: Shutterstock/Lesia Povkh; pp4-5: Shutterstock/Katja Tsvetkova; pp6-7: Shutterstock/Smileus; p7t: Shutterstock/Kit Korzun; p7bl: Shutterstock/Alexandr Junek Imaging; p7b: Shutterstock/Jurgen Vogt; p7br: Shutterstock/Slowmotiongli; p8: Shutterstock/PhotocechCZ; p9t: Shutterstock/Sergey Uryadnikov; pp10-11: Shutterstock/Onyx9; p12: Shutterstock/Albie Venter; p13t: Shutterstock/Tadan; p13c: Shutterstock/TravellingFatman; p13b: Shutterstock/Gene Sizemore Photography; pp14-15: Shutterstock/Lesia Povkh; pp16-17: Shutterstock/Marian Galovic; p16c: Shutterstock/Ground Picture; p16b: Shutterstock/Ground Picture; pp18-19: Shutterstock/Ayotography; p19b: Shutterstock/D.Cz.; p20: Shutterstock/Gudkov Andrey; p21t: Shutterstock/Jiri Hrebicek; p21c: Shutterstock/Christian Musat; p21b: Shutterstock/Tony Campbell; pp22-23: Shutterstock/Asaf Weizman; p23t: Shutterstock/Motortion Films; p23b: Shutterstock/Motortion Films; pp24-25: Shutterstock/Fiona Ayerst; p25: Shutterstock/Travel Stock; pp26-27: Shutterstock/Nelio Pereira; p27t: Shutterstock/Nick Fox; p27c: Shutterstock/Claire E Carter; p27b: Shutterstock/Travelling Fatman; pp28-29: Shutterstock/Brina L. Bunt; p29r: Shutterstock/OlegRi; p29t: Shutterstock/Tiplyashina Evgeniya; p29b: Shutterstock/Tiplyashina Evgeniya; pp30-31: Shutterstock/Martin Prochazkacz; p31: Shutterstock/Toa55; pp32-33: Shutterstock/Kiki Dohmeier; p33t: Shutterstock/Vagabondering Andy; p33c: Shutterstock/Boleslaw Kubica; pp34-35: Shutterstock/Claudio Soldi; p35t: Shutterstock/Ground Picture; p35b: Shutterstock/Ground Picture; pp36-37: Shutterstock/Albert Beukhof; p37b: Shutterstock/Emily Marie Wilson; p38t: Shutterstock/Abeselom Zerit; p38b: Shutterstock/Sergey Uryadnikov; p39b: Shutterstock/Everything I Do; pp40-41: Shutterstock/Vladimir Turkenich; p40t: Shutterstock/Robert Kneschke; p40b: Shutterstock/Robert Kneschke; p42: Shutterstock/Gorodenkoff; p43: Shutterstock/Jurgens Potgieter; p44: Shutterstock/GaudiLab; p45: Shutterstock/Sergey Uryadnikov.

Printed in China

Publisher's Note: The information in the Kids on a Mission features in this book are suggestions for actions that children can take to help protect endangered animals, based on extensive research by the author and consultant. The email addresses and the children featured in the photographs are for illustrative purposes only.

CONTENTS

GORILLAS IN DANGER

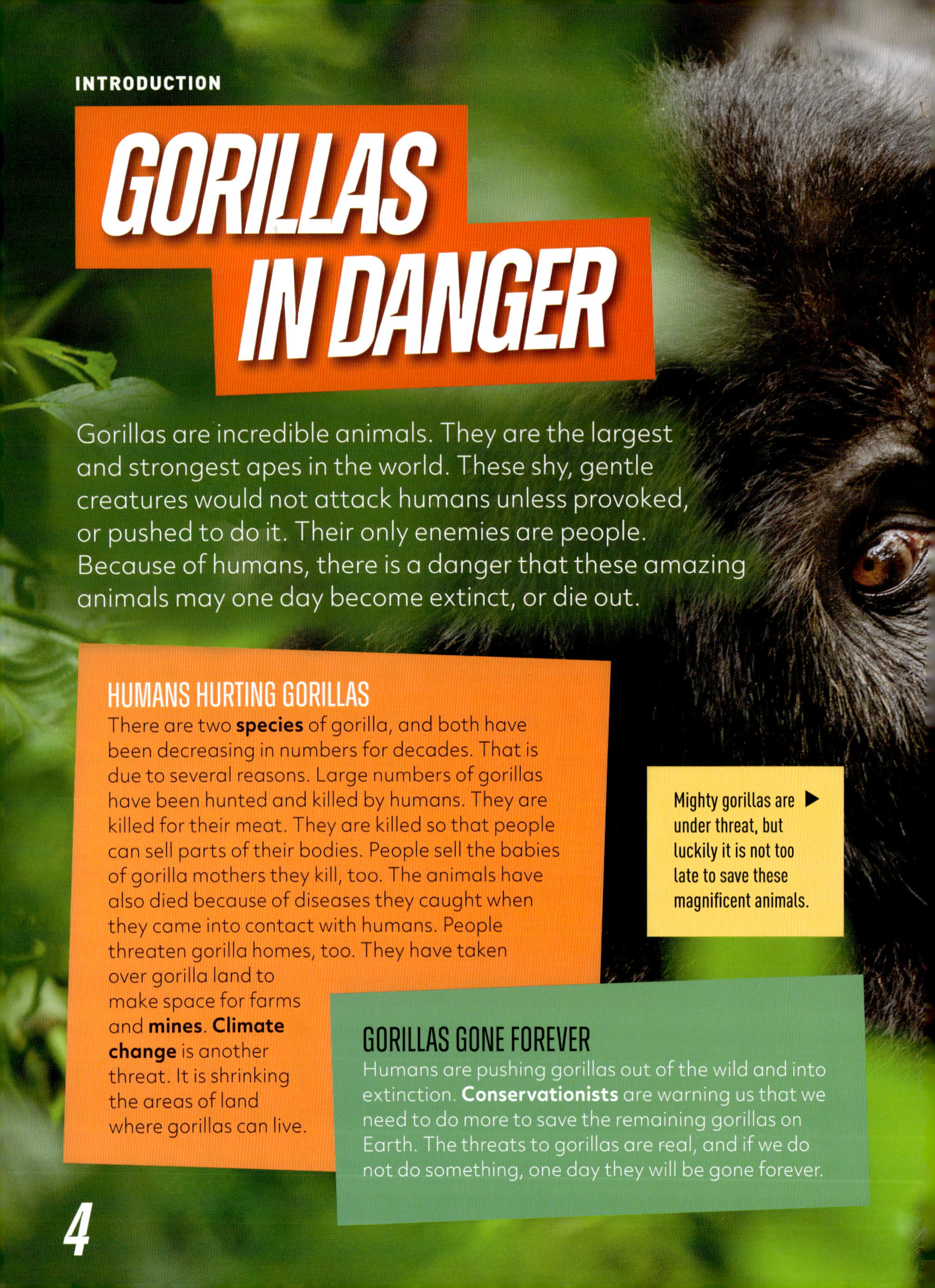

Gorillas are incredible animals. They are the largest and strongest apes in the world. These shy, gentle creatures would not attack humans unless provoked, or pushed to do it. Their only enemies are people. Because of humans, there is a danger that these amazing animals may one day become extinct, or die out.

HUMANS HURTING GORILLAS

There are two **species** of gorilla, and both have been decreasing in numbers for decades. That is due to several reasons. Large numbers of gorillas have been hunted and killed by humans. They are killed for their meat. They are killed so that people can sell parts of their bodies. People sell the babies of gorilla mothers they kill, too. The animals have also died because of diseases they caught when they came into contact with humans. People threaten gorilla homes, too. They have taken over gorilla land to make space for farms and **mines**. **Climate change** is another threat. It is shrinking the areas of land where gorillas can live.

Mighty gorillas are ▶ under threat, but luckily it is not too late to save these magnificent animals.

GORILLAS GONE FOREVER

Humans are pushing gorillas out of the wild and into extinction. **Conservationists** are warning us that we need to do more to save the remaining gorillas on Earth. The threats to gorillas are real, and if we do not do something, one day they will be gone forever.

"Gorillas are actually special, special animals. We need to protect them, so that they live forever."

Jean Paul Hirwa, gorilla program manager,
Dian Fossey Gorilla Fund

HELP THE GORILLA!

There is still hope for the gorilla, and it is not too late to save it. People everywhere have heard the gorilla's call for help. And they are making it their mission to help these amazing animals survive. In this book, we'll learn about the gorilla and why it is in danger. We'll discover what people are doing to help gorillas and how they have built a career in **conservation**. We'll find out how kids everywhere can make it their mission to help save the gorilla. And we'll learn how you could make a career in conservation your mission. Feeling mission-ready? Then read on!

The International Union for Conservation of Nature (IUCN) keeps a record of the world's species and how at risk of extinction they are. It is called the **Red List.**

There are more than **142,500** species on the Red List.

The gorilla is one of the most **endangered** animals in the world.

CHAPTER ONE

MEET THE GORILLA

Gorillas are known as gentle giants. That is because, although these animals are huge, they are actually very calm and peaceful.

MIGHTY MALES

Male gorillas can be twice as big as the females. An adult male gorilla measures up to 6 feet (1.8 m) tall when standing on two feet. That's as tall as an adult man. It can weigh up to 550 pounds (250 kg), which is as heavy as three adult men! Older male gorillas are known as silverbacks because their back hair turns silvery gray with age.

TIP TO TOES

Gorillas have thick, dark hair over most of their body. Only the face, chest, palms of the hands, and soles of the feet are hairless. Gorillas have long, muscular arms and short back legs. Gorillas can walk upright, but they usually walk around on all fours, resting on the knuckles.

LIKE PEOPLE

A gorilla has 10 fingers on its humanlike hands and 10 toes on its feet. The gorilla has small ears on the side of its head. It has small eyes, large nostrils, and a hairless face. The gorilla shares many features with humans—it can see, hear, and smell like people do.

GORILLA GROUPS

Gorillas live in groups called troops. They can be made up of between two and 40 animals. Within this group, there is one male who is in charge. He is called the dominant male. There are also several adult females and their young. The dominant male decides where to find food and protects the females and young.

In a Group

Scientists group animals to help classify, or order, them. Gorillas belong to a group of animals called Gorilla. The group has two species: western and eastern gorillas. These are divided into four **subspecies**. The two subspecies of western gorillas are western lowland gorillas and Cross River gorillas. The two species of eastern gorillas are eastern lowland gorillas (or Grauer's gorillas) and mountain gorillas.

WHERE GORILLAS LIVE

All gorillas live in remote, or faraway, forests in Africa. Western and eastern gorillas are separated by a huge wilderness area that is about 560 miles (almost 900 km) wide. It is called the Congo River Basin.

WESTERN GORILLAS

Each gorilla species is separated into two subspecies: one that lives in uplands and the other that lives in lowlands. The Cross River gorilla is found only in high **montane rain forests** and **bamboo** forests in a few patches in Nigeria and Cameroon. Western lowland gorillas are found in the huge lowland rain forests and swamp forests of central Africa.

EASTERN GORILLAS

Mountain gorillas live in high montane and bamboo forests in two separate locations. The first is the Virunga mountain range, found on the borders of the Democratic Republic of Congo (DRC), Rwanda, and Uganda. It also lives in the Bwindi Impenetrable National Park in Uganda. Eastern lowland gorillas live in **tropical** rain forests in the DRC.

▲ The eastern lowland gorilla is the biggest of the gorilla subspecies. This mighty animal has a stocky body, large hands, and a short muzzle.

If challenged, male ▶ western lowland gorillas may roar to show they are powerful.

▲ Much of the land gorillas once lived on has been taken over by humans.

LOSING LAND

The number of gorillas that remain in the wild varies between subspecies. The Cross River gorilla is the world's rarest great ape. The 300 that are left live only in the upland border between Nigeria and Cameroon. The western lowland gorilla is the most widespread and numerous of the four gorilla subspecies. It is protected by the thick, swampy forests where it lives. There are around only 1,000 mountain gorillas left. The spread of humans has forced mountain gorillas farther up into the mountains for longer periods. That has made them endure dangerous and sometimes deadly conditions. There are fewer than 4,000 eastern lowland gorillas left in the wild. Studies suggest that they live on only 13 percent of the land where they once lived.

WHY SHOULD WE HELP THE GORILLA?

Gorillas are incredibly important to the environments in which they live. Without these huge grazing animals, the health of their forest **habitats** would be disrupted. That could be damaging for other wildlife and people in the area, too.

GORILLA GARDENERS

Gorillas eat a lot of fruit and swallow the seeds inside the fruit. The seeds pass through the gorilla's digestive system whole and come out hours later in poop. Because gorillas move around, the seeds that come out in gorilla poop are dropped far from the trees on which they grew. Around half the seeds are dropped near gorilla nesting sites. They are places where gorillas make nests in which to rest. They are usually in areas of forest that have plenty of light. That gives the seeds a better chance of growing into healthy new trees. An added bonus is that the gorilla poop acts like **fertilizer** and helps the plants grow.

NOT JUST THE GORILLA

By protecting gorilla habitat, we are helping all the other plants and animals that live there. Many different **organisms** live in the mountains on which gorillas are found. If these places are kept healthy for gorillas, they are kept healthy for every other organism that lives there, too. Protecting gorillas also helps people! The habitats in which gorillas live also provide people with food. They also include plants that can be used for medicines, as well as wood for shelter, heat, and fuel.

◀ Gorillas depend on the forest for food and a place to live and raise their young, but in turn, the gorillas' ecosystem depends on gorillas.

What Is an Ecosystem?

An ecosystem is a group of natural parts that all work together for a purpose. Ecosystems include nonliving things such as water, sunshine, and air. These are called abiotic factors. Ecosystems also include living things such as plants and animals. These are called biotic factors. The living things in an ecosystem depend on the abiotic factors in the ecosystem to survive. Every part of the ecosystem has an important part to play. A healthy ecosystem has many different plants and animals living together. If any part of that ecosystem changes or is damaged, the other parts are affected, too.

GORILLA—A GIANT APPETITE

Gorillas eat mainly plants. An adult male eats up to 40 pounds (18 kg) of food each day. Gorillas have a great big stomach to hold all the food that they eat!

ON THE MENU

Gorillas eat a variety of plants, depending on where they live. They eat leaves, roots, fruit, and even tree bark. Some gorilla species eat more than 200 different types of plants and fruit. Gorillas also sometimes eat worms, ants, and **termites**.

FINDING FOOD

Gorillas have good eyesight, which they use to find food. They also have good hearing. That helps them tell each other where food is when they are among thick forest plants. Strong jaws help gorillas chew tough stems.

FINGER FOOD

Like humans, gorillas can press their thumb against a finger to pick up small things. That means they can use their fingers to collect, peel, and prepare food. Occasionally, they use tools to get food. For example, they may use a stick to catch ants.

SLOW EATERS

Gorillas spend about one-third of their day eating. Plant foods are not very rich in some nutrients, or goodness. So gorillas must eat a lot to get the nutrients they need.

PEOPLE ON A MISSION

Gorillas face some serious threats. However, many people are trying to help them. Some work in conservation. They are on a mission to protect gorillas. They want to secure a safe future for these gentle giants.

PEOPLE IN OFFICES

People who work in conservation organizations help develop rules and guidance about conservation actions. They work with the governments in countries where gorillas live. Together, they come up with plans to protect the gorillas and their habitats. There are also charities in which people raise money to save gorillas. **Communications** and public relations experts help organizations raise awareness about gorillas.

PEOPLE ON THE GROUND

People work on the ground in the wild to protect the gorilla and its habitat. Wildlife managers, rangers, and officers are conservationists who work in places where the gorilla lives. They help protect the animal's home and monitor its numbers. Wildlife technicians collect data, or information, on wildlife and habitats and often work alongside a wildlife manager. Public educators and outreach specialists work with people to help educate them about gorillas. They encourage people to protect gorillas and make their homes a safer place in which to live.

PEOPLE IN THE LAB

Zoology is the study of animal life. Zoologists are scientists who study gorillas and other animals in labs, zoos, and in the wild. They study their behavior and intelligence. They may write books or articles on the animals. Conservationists use this information to help them protect gorillas in the wild.

▼ Wildlife rangers wear face masks when near gorillas to keep the animals from catching diseases.

MAKE IT YOUR MISSION

You could help gorillas and other endangered animals by taking action and planning a career in conservation. Here's how:

1. In this book, you'll discover what actions kids on a mission can take to help gorillas. Use them to inspire your own actions to rescue gorillas.
2. You'll also discover some of the careers people on a mission have in gorilla conservation. As you read about each one, think about whether that career in conservation might suit you.
3. At the end of this book, you'll find a guide to how to build a career in conservation. Check it out to discover how you can make saving animals your life mission.

PEOPLE EVERYWHERE

Ordinary people everywhere, including kids just like you, raise money to save gorillas. They share information they learn about threats gorillas face with their friends and family. They join organizations that aim to help gorillas.

CHAPTER TWO

HOMES UNDER THREAT

There are now more people on Earth than ever before. Africa, the **continent** on which gorillas live, has one of the fastest-growing **populations** in the world. And all those people need space to live, grow food, and work. That is creating more demand for the land and **resources** that gorillas rely on.

DESTROYING FORESTS

Local people cut or burn forests to clear land for homes. They also clear it to grow crops or raise livestock. They cut down trees to get wood for firewood, charcoal, and building materials. The charcoal may be sold on to **traders**, who then sell it to people in cities for fuel for heating and cooking. Many of the local people who cut down trees are poor. The money they get from the timber, or cut-down trees, is their only means of survival. In contrast, big **logging** companies sell the timber for a lot of money.

Kids on a Mission

@zoolily_2006

To help reduce the demand for mining in gorilla habitat, I try not to buy new cell phones and other electronic gadgets too often. I send old ones to recycling programs instead of dumping them, too.

TAKING OVER LAND

Mining also causes habitat loss. Mines are dug to extract, or take out, valuable metals and **minerals**, such as gold and coltan. Coltan is a type of **ore** that is used in cell phones and other electronic devices. It helps them store electricity. Around 80 percent of the world's coltan is found in eastern lowland gorilla and mountain gorilla habitats. Mining is illegal in some of these areas. However, the mines are in remote places and often guarded by armed workers. That makes it difficult to make people follow laws there.

▲ Forest homes provide gorillas with shelter, food, and a place to raise young.

KEEPING GORILLAS SAFE

To protect gorillas, conservationists have set up wildlife reserves. They are areas in which gorillas should be safe from threats such as logging. Wildlife reserves are monitored by people working in gorilla conservation, who try and keep the gorillas there safe. Conservationists also create wildlife corridors for the gorillas. They are stretches of land that connect two wildlife reserves. They give gorillas the chance to move safely between important habitats. Unfortunately, only 17 percent of gorillas currently live in protected areas.

> "The mountain gorilla faces extinction ... because of the **encroachments** of ... man upon its habitat."
>
> Dian Fossey, world-famous zoologist and gorilla expert

SPOTLIGHT ON LOGGING

Logging is a big problem for gorillas because timber is a major export in central Africa. An export is a good that is made in one country and then sold to another. When forests are cut down and the wood is dragged away to sell as timber, gorillas have nowhere left to live and find food.

LOSING OUT TO LOGGERS

Logging workers use bulldozers, trucks, and other heavy earth-removing machinery to make roads. They use the roads to reach remote areas of forest. They cut down the trees and remove the branches from tree trunks. They then transport the timber from the forest. The large-scale roadbuilding, noise, and loss of trees have a terrible effect on gorillas.

GORILLAS IN TROUBLE

Gorillas are shy and nervous around people. The noise from heavy machinery alone is enough to push them into smaller areas farther away from human activity. When roads are carved through their forest homes, it keeps gorillas from traveling between areas to find food and **mates**. An even worse problem is that logging roads have opened up huge areas of gorilla habitat to hunters and farmers. That means they can reach more remote places and clear more land.

PEOPLE ON A MISSION: GORILLA SUPPORT

Wildlife **policy** analysts and consultants work with governments and timber companies to encourage the use of good environmental practices in the logging industry. They push companies to take on the Forest Stewardship Council (FSC) certification. That tells people that the wood, paper, and other forest products they buy are responsibly sourced, or taken.

Specialists work with local communities to try and stop people from cutting down so many trees. In times of war, when people entered gorilla reserves to escape danger, specialists gave them emergency wood for fuel. That kept the people from cutting down trees. Specialists also work with local people to help them plant more trees to reforest areas. Reforesting means the planting of new trees to replace those that have been cut down.

Ecotourism is where people pay to visit a wild place to see its plants and animals. Ecotourist specialists train local people to take care of travelers who come to see gorillas in their natural habitat. Local people can earn more from tourism than they can by cutting down trees. That has helped protect the forests and the mountain gorillas. Money earned from tourism is also used to protect the habitat that people and the gorillas rely on.

◀ Logging companies have the tools and equipment to quickly cut down and remove many huge trees from a forest.

Around 80 percent of gorillas live in unprotected areas. They are at risk from human activities in their habitat. ▶

LIVING WITH THE GORILLA

The forests of Africa are home to a variety of amazing animals. People love to visit Africa to see its spectacular wildlife, such as its lions, giraffes, and elephants. Sadly, like the gorilla, many of Africa's incredible animals are also in danger of dying out.

THE AFRICAN FOREST ELEPHANT

The African forest elephant is the smaller of the two African elephant species. It has straighter and thinner tusks. It also has rounder ears, and its skull is a different shape. These elephants live in swampy areas during the dry season. They move back to lowland rain forest in the wet season. They feed on trees, shrubs, grasses, herbs, and fruits. They are under threat because of habitat loss. They are also illegally hunted for their **ivory** tusks. They are killed by farmers for eating crops and trampling them, too.

THE OKAPI

The okapi looks like a cross between a deer and a zebra. However, it is known as the "forest giraffe," because it's the giraffe's only living relative. The okapi has very large, upright ears that can pick up the slightest sounds. It has a long, dark tongue. It uses it to strip the buds and young leaves from plants in its rain forest home. Its stripes provide **camouflage** when the animal stands in the rays of sunlight that shine through rain forest trees.

THE CONGO PEAFOWL

The Congo peafowl is the national bird of the DRC. These chicken-sized birds can fly, but only for a short time. Males have a white crest of head feathers. Their dark-blue body feathers have patches of metallic green and purple. Females have a brown front with shiny bright green feathers on the back. Their lowland rain forest habitat is threatened by mining, logging, and farming. People also hunt the birds and take their eggs.

THE GOLDEN MONKEY

The golden monkey gets its name for its striking coloring. These monkeys live in high bamboo forests. They depend completely on bamboo forests. They eat mainly bamboo shoots and leaves. They weave nests from bamboo, where they sleep. Any threat to bamboo is a threat to the golden monkey. The animals are endangered because bamboo forests are being destroyed.

CHAPTER THREE

UNDER THREAT FROM POACHING

Poaching is the illegal killing or capture of animals. Poachers kill gorillas for their meat. The bushmeat trade is mostly illegal. Bushmeat is meat from wild animals. However, some people are ready to risk getting caught because they need the money. Poaching is often their only source of money.

EASY POACHING

Poachers get into remote forests more easily now because they can use roads built by logging companies. Poachers can use logging roads to reach much deeper into the rain forest to find more gorillas. They also often use logging vehicles to transport bushmeat to sell in faraway markets.

EASY TARGETS

Gorillas are relatively easy to kill. They live mostly on the ground and in relatively large groups. That means that they can be easily tracked and hunted for bushmeat. Gorillas are a prized source of bushmeat. They are so large that killing one animal can provide a lot of meat. Poachers also lay iron **snares** to catch other animals, and gorillas can be accidentally killed or badly injured by the traps.

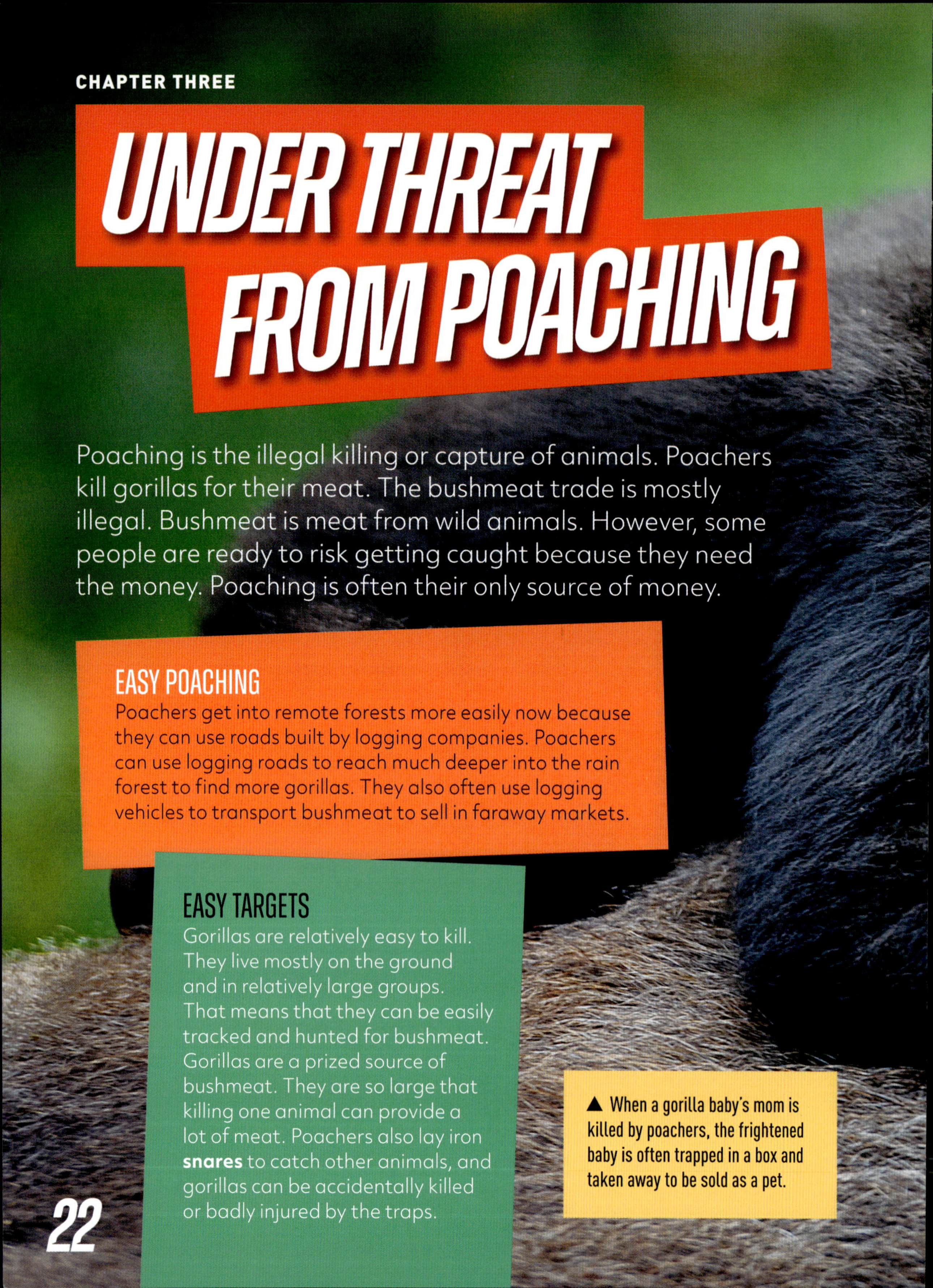

▲ When a gorilla baby's mom is killed by poachers, the frightened baby is often trapped in a box and taken away to be sold as a pet.

"People have even found gorillas (being eaten) in Belgium, and I know of cases in London."

Andrew Plumptre, the Wildlife Conservation Society (WCS)

Kids on a Mission

@No-poaching_12

I held a sponsored run for gorillas this year. I got all my friends involved, too. We donated the money we made to a wildlife charity that protects gorillas.

PETS AND SOUVENIRS

Gorilla babies are too small to sell for bushmeat, so when poachers kill gorilla mothers, they may take the babies and try to sell them as pets. Many such babies die of stress, hunger, **neglect**, and disease. Some gorillas are hunted for their body parts. They are used in traditional medicines. Hands, skulls, and feet are sold illegally as **souvenirs** or lucky charms.

SPOTLIGHT ON BUSHMEAT

The trade in bushmeat takes place throughout west and central Africa. It is one of the biggest threats facing gorillas today.

Large male silverbacks ▶ protect their troop. When they're killed, the rest of the troop may be at risk.

FEEDING FAMILIES, MAKING MONEY

In the past, local people caught gorillas for bushmeat to feed their families. They only caught what they needed to survive. Today, the sale of bushmeat is a growing industry, and bushmeat can be exported around the world. It means that many more gorillas are killed for the bushmeat trade. As well as being sold to workers in logging companies and mines, gorilla bushmeat is sold as a luxury food product in other countries.

DEADLY TO GORILLAS

Shooting gorillas for bushmeat has a devastating impact on gorilla populations. Gorillas **reproduce** slowly. That means that even a small amount of poaching can cause a drop in gorilla numbers that can take many years to recover from. If a large male silverback gorilla leader is killed, the rest of his troop may split up. That puts the gorillas at risk of attacks from other male gorillas. Leopards may also then attack them.

▼ Rangers put their lives on the line every day. Many rangers have been killed when they have tried to stop armed poachers from killing gorillas.

PEOPLE ON A MISSION: GORILLA PROTECTORS

Wildlife rangers work in different ways to protect the gorilla and prevent poaching for bushmeat. They patrol large areas of land where gorillas are protected. They watch out for illegal activities. They track and stop poachers. They have the power to arrest them. They can take away any bushmeat and weapons the poachers may have.

Wildlife rangers also work to create stronger **boundaries** around protected areas to keep poachers from getting in. They cut or clear away wire snare animal traps that they find. They also save injured gorillas. They carry out studies to monitor the gorillas' health and collect vital conservation data.

Rangers talk to local people about why hunting for bushmeat is so harmful to gorillas. They educate local children who could one day be tempted to hunt for bushmeat, too. They discuss things that local people could do to earn money instead. They try and help them find alternatives to eating wild bushmeat. They include wild meat from **sustainable** hunting or **domestication** of wild animals.

GORILLA BABIES

A female gorilla gives birth to between just three and four babies over her entire lifetime. One or two of those babies will not make it to adulthood. This low rate of reproduction makes it difficult for gorillas to recover from population declines.

GORILLA MOMS

A gorilla is pregnant for around eight and a half months before she gives birth. Like humans, female gorillas usually give birth to one baby at a time. They may sometimes have twins. Gorilla babies weigh about 4.5 pounds (2 kg) at birth. They have pale gray-pink skin and thin hair.

NURSING MOMS

Moms do most of the childcare. A gorilla mom nurses her baby, or feeds it with milk from her body. She nurses for up to two and a half years. Babies start eating some plants at around three months old and eat mostly plants from seven months. After babies stop nursing, they may stay close to their mother for years.

CARRYING BABY

A gorilla mom carries her baby for the first few months. She holds the baby close to her chest. The baby grips the mother's hair tightly with its hands and feet. Later, the baby starts to ride on its mom's back.

GORILLA PLAY

Baby gorillas usually begin playing, smiling, and bouncing at eight weeks. At about nine weeks, they begin crawling. Young gorillas like to play with their older brothers and sisters and other youngsters in their troop. They wrestle, tumble, climb trees, and march together through the forest. That helps them to build strength. It also teaches them to climb well.

CHAPTER FOUR

THE THREAT OF CLIMATE CHANGE

Gorillas face many threats, from hunting and farming through mining and logging. But the biggest threat of all to these majestic animals may be Earth's changing climate. In the forests where gorillas live, climate change is having a dangerous impact.

WHAT IS CLIMATE CHANGE?

Climate change is a change in temperature or weather in an area over a long period of time. Climate change has always happened slowly throughout Earth's history, due to natural factors such as changes in the sun and **geological** activity. However, the climate change we are experiencing today is largely caused by human activities. These include burning **fossil fuels**, which releases gases into Earth's **atmosphere**. These gases circle the planet like a blanket, causing it to heat up.

"As climate change forces vegetation uphill … all animals—not only great apes – that depend on particular habitat types will be forced to move uphill or become locally extinct."

Fiona Maisels, WCS

◀ Heatwaves and droughts are major threats to the health of Africa's forests.

RISING TEMPERATURES, DEADLY DROUGHTS, AND FIERCE FIRES

Climate change results in much hotter temperatures in some places. It increases the risk of heatwaves and makes them hotter and longer. A heatwave is a long spell of high temperatures. The extra heat sucks water out of plants and soil. That leaves trees and other plants so dry that they easily catch fire. That causes wildfires, which can rage for weeks and burn a lot of trees and other plants. Climate change also changes rainfall patterns. Long periods of dry weather when it hardly rains are called droughts. Droughts can be disastrous for plants, because they need water to survive. In a drought, many plants dry up and die.

Kids on a Mission

@lulu4apes_2008

My family and I travel by train when we can. Instead of flying abroad for vacations, we enjoy staycations in our home country.

▲ Planes travel high up in the atmosphere, so the gases that they release have an even greater effect on climate change.

SPOTLIGHT ON HEATWAVES AND DROUGHTS

Gorillas rely on their forest homes. Changes to those forests could prove disastrous for these gentle giants.

SHRINKING HABITATS

Climate change will make some lowlands hotter, drier, and less suitable for lowland gorillas to live in. Some lowland gorillas may be able to move to higher ground. But this may be impossible if there are no wildlife corridors through which to travel or if there is no high ground nearby. In that case, the gorillas will be left with nowhere to go.

Gorillas are big animals ▶ that need a lot of food, but climate change is reducing their food supplies.

FOREST THREATS

Climate change increases the risk of forest fires, which destroy gorilla habitat. Gorillas may also struggle to cope with heatwaves and could get sick because of the heat. Heatwaves and drought will reduce the gorillas' water and food supplies. They will also affect the food and water supplies of people living nearby. This will mean that people may then enter more gorilla areas to find resources.

PEOPLE ON A MISSION: FIGHTING CLIMATE CHANGE

Some people are on a mission to help gorillas survive climate change. These people are trying to deal with the threat that climate change poses to gorillas and their forest homes.

Some scientists are studying gorillas to find out how vulnerable the animals are to climate change. They look at how well the species could adapt to changing conditions. For example, gorillas do not need large areas of water, and they feed on a wide variety of food. That should mean that they could survive in new areas if they had to move due to climate change. However, if they move, that may increase conflict with humans. It will also put the gorillas at risk of catching human illnesses. Some scientists monitor gorilla diseases. They look at ways to increase gorilla habitats or **relocate** gorillas to safe areas, away from humans.

Some people work for organizations that produce commercials or online features that tell the public about the threat of climate change and its effect on wildlife. They show people that by making choices that have less harmful effects on the environment, they can help reduce climate change. These organizations also work with scientists to find information they can use to persuade governments and businesses to take action to prevent more climate change.

▲ Once a fire starts in a warm, dry forest, the flames burn through the trees at a frightening pace.

GORILLAS NEED FOREST PLANTS

Gorillas are adapted to the forests in which they live. That means that their bodies and behavior have changed to suit their environment. They rely on the plants in forests for everything they need. That includes food, shelter, and water.

DRINKING WATER

Gorillas do not usually drink water from lakes or streams. As well as getting food from plants, gorillas get all of the moisture they need from their food. They also get it from morning dew that collects on forest plants.

NESTS FOR THE NIGHT

Every evening, gorillas bend branches and leaves to make a sleeping nest on the ground or in the trees. They build a new nest every night. After a morning of feeding, adult gorillas gather leaves, twigs, and branches to make a day nest for resting while the youngsters play.

GOING UP

A gorilla's body is adapted for life among forest plants. It can use its strong front arms to help it climb trees to get food or nest. Larger gorillas take care when climbing—they are so heavy that they can break thin branches!

GEARED UP GORILLAS

Mountain gorillas are perfectly adapted for high mountain forests. They have thicker fur, and more of it, than the other gorillas. That helps them survive in mountain forests where temperatures often drop below freezing.

CHAPTER FIVE

OTHER THREATS TO GORILLAS

One reason that people love gorillas and want to save them is that they are so similar to us. People want to visit gorilla habitats to be near the animals. But that closeness causes problems for gorillas. Catching diseases from people is a major threat to these creatures.

DEADLY DISEASE

As more people move into their habitat and more tourists come to see them, more gorillas are getting exposed to different human diseases. When people come into contact with gorillas, they can pass on diseases to the animals. Gorillas that catch a disease from humans can be more badly affected by the disease than the people. For example, mountain gorillas can die from just a common cold.

Diseases can be passed to gorillas by contact with poachers, loggers, and miners. Diseases can also be caught when people create homes or farms on the edge of gorilla habitat. The trade in bushmeat brings the most frequent contact.

▼ People love to see gorillas. However, tourism can put gorillas at risk of catching diseases.

"If we don't start dealing with the disease threats, then the conservation outlook for these species is very dim."

Peter Walsh, ecologist at Cambridge University, United Kingdom (UK)

Kids on a Mission

@gogogorillagirl–07

I chose to do a research paper on gorillas for a school project. I showed it to all my classmates. Now they are helping gorillas by telling their families and friends, too.

USED TO PEOPLE

There is also an increased danger when gorillas get used to humans. For example, the animals may become used to seeing tourist groups and lose their fear of them. Tourism should not be a problem if rules to protect the gorillas are strictly followed. Unfortunately, that is not always the case.

FIGHTING AND GORILLAS

Armed conflict in Africa has greatly affected gorillas. Today, many of the conflicts are between armed groups fighting to get valuable mineral resources and control mines. That creates more habitat loss and poaching. It also increases the risk of passing on diseases.

SPOTLIGHT ON DISEASES

Gorillas are closely related to humans. In fact, they share 98 percent of the same **deoxyribonucleic acid (DNA)**. The reason that gorillas can so easily catch human diseases is that they share so many of our characteristics. Of course, this works both ways. Many human outbreaks of disease have started after people came into contact with infected gorilla bodies or bushmeat.

A DEADLY VIRUS

Some diseases that are passed on to gorilla populations are deadly. Ebola virus is a particularly nasty example. This virus causes internal bleeding that can kill humans and great apes. The disease is extremely deadly for gorillas. If they are infected, there is a 90 to 98 percent chance that they will die. In 2004, Ebola killed 95 percent of western lowland gorillas living in the Odzala-Kokoua National Park, DRC.

Scientists believe that Ebola has ▲ wiped out around one-third of the world's gorillas during the past 40 years.

PEOPLE ON A MISSION: GORILLA SCIENTISTS

Zoologists conduct research in labs, universities, and other organizations. They study gorillas to find out more about them, such as what they eat and how they raise their young. Zoologists study diseases the animals suffer from and ways they can help them.

Zoologists also work in wildlife reserves. There, they monitor changes in gorilla populations and health, and they study the animals' behavior. They set up gorilla health programs to reduce the risk of diseases among gorillas. They anesthetize gorillas, or put them to sleep for a while. They are then able to remove snares and treat wounds safely. They monitor outbreaks of diseases and advise on actions, such as keeping people from moving between an Ebola outbreak area and a gorilla area.

Scientists in labs study gorilla **genetics** and work on new medicines that could help gorillas. They have developed a **vaccine** that could prevent the Ebola virus from killing gorillas. The challenge they face is how to give wild gorillas the vaccine. Some scientists are working on smart ways of doing that. For example, the vaccine may be hidden in food. It may also be attached to another, harmless virus that could spread from gorilla to gorilla.

◀ Vets called gorilla doctors give sick gorillas medicines to treat life-threatening infections.

OTHER GREAT APES IN DANGER

Around the world, other great apes are in danger. Many of them face similar challenges to the gorilla. They are also rapidly losing much of their forest habitat to human activities such as farming, mining, and logging.

THE BONOBO

The bonobo lives in tropical forests in the DRC. Bonobos are similar to chimpanzees, but bonobos have longer legs, shorter arms, and a narrower trunk. They are also generally smaller. They have a round skull, a flat black face, and red lips. Bonobos live in large groups of up to 120 animals.

THE CHIMPANZEE

Chimpanzees live all over Africa, from the west coast to as far east as western Uganda, Rwanda, Burundi, and Tanzania. They are found in rain forests, open woodlands, and bamboo forests. They also live in swamp forests and even open **savanna** near patches of forest. Chimpanzees spend a lot of time in the treetops. They mostly walk on all fours when on the ground. They eat plant parts and insects, but they sometimes hunt monkeys or small antelopes for meat. Habitat loss, poaching, and disease are major threats to the chimpanzee.

THE ORANGUTAN

Orangutans live in the rain forests of Borneo and Sumatra. These islands are found in Indonesia. The orangutan is the only great ape found outside of Africa. The name *orangutan* means "man of the forest," and orangutans spend almost all their time in the trees. They use their long, powerful arms and grasping hands and feet to swing through the branches. These red-haired great apes are under threat from habitat loss and hunting. In the rain forests of Indonesia, their homes are being destroyed in wildfires caused by increasing periods of drought.

WHAT'S NEXT FOR THE GORILLA?

Gorillas and their habitats face a number of very serious threats. The good news is that all over the world ordinary people, conservationists, and governments are working hard to ensure the survival of this magnificent animal.

HELP FROM CONSERVATIONISTS

Conservationists are educating people who live near gorilla habitats about why the animals need to be protected. They work with local people to reduce poaching and killing gorillas for bushmeat. They teach people how to protect gorillas. For example, they explain how to keep diseases from spreading through improved hygiene, such as handwashing. Conservationists help improve local people's lives. They may provide tanks in which people can collect rainwater. That means that they don't need to go into gorilla forests for water. Conservationists also work with governments to make stronger laws that prevent the illegal trade in bushmeat and the threat from illegal mining.

Kids on a Mission

@primate_nate_06

I'm working hard in all my science subjects. I hope to be a zoologist or vet one day, so I can find new ways of saving the gorilla.

> *"Surely, we do not want to live in a world without the great apes, our closest living relatives in the animal kingdom?"*
>
> Jane Goodall, world-famous conservationist

HELP FROM ORGANIZATIONS

The World Wildlife Fund (WWF) is one of the organizations fighting to save gorillas. Today, less than 20 percent of gorillas live in protected regions. The WWF is working to create new or bigger protected areas for gorillas in many places. In Cameroon, the organization is helping to set up gorilla sanctuaries, or safe places, to keep the rare Cross River gorilla and the western lowland gorilla safe. The WWF is also getting groups of gorillas used to humans. This will mean that tourists can visit gorilla areas. The money raised from tourism will pay for the protection of gorillas and their homes.

HELP FROM ALL OF US

Everyone, everywhere can help save the gorilla. We can all live, travel, eat, and shop in more sustainable ways to reduce the threat of climate change. We can learn more about gorilla threats, so that we can raise awareness of the issues. By working together, it is possible to save the gorilla. Already, the hard work is paying off. Recently, the number of mountain gorillas alone has been rising. In the future, hopefully we will see populations of all four types of gorillas increasing. One day, all of these magnificent animals may finally be safe.

MAKE IT YOUR MISSION: A CAREER IN CONSERVATION

Why not make it your mission to build a future career in conservation? That way, you could make a huge difference to gorillas and other endangered animals. On pages 44–45 you'll find some of the conservation careers you could pursue. And here are things you can do right now to prepare for a career in conservation and help save gorillas.

GET SET TO STUDY

Working hard at school now will pay off if you want a conservation career. Pay attention in your science, English, and geography classes. Languages are also useful. If you have a job oversees, being able to speak a foreign language is helpful.

Working hard in your science ▶ class will help you build a future career in conservation.

GET EXPERIENCE

Any form of work experience in wildlife care will be useful for a future conservation career. Why not apply to local zoos, charities, and conservation organizations as soon as you are old enough?

▲ Adopting a gorilla is a great way to help protect the animal and its species.

TAKE ACTION!

You have learned about some of the actions that help gorillas from the Kids on a Mission features in this book. Here are some more ideas for other activities that can help protect gorillas:

- Avoid updating your cell phone too often, and recycle it to reduce the impact of coltan mining.
- Ask your parents to buy furniture and wooden items that are FSC certified. This means that the wood comes from forests that are sustainably managed.
- Adopt a gorilla! Ask your parents to help you check out the WWF site for information about adopting gorillas.
- Choose FSC-certified or recycled tissue and toilet paper. These products are not made from paper from trees cut down in rain forests.
- Ask your school to hold a fundraising event to raise money for an organization such as WWF to help them protect gorillas.
- Start a blog about gorillas and the dangers they face. Educate as many people as you can.

GET CONNECTED

Connecting with other people who care about wildlife is a great way to feel empowered about saving endangered animals. You'll find some of the organizations you can join on page 47. By connecting with other people who are concerned about the environment, you'll find out what you can do to help. Being involved with conservation organizations and charities now will also help you when you apply for jobs in the future. It will show that you have been interested in conservation from an early age.

CAREERS IN CONSERVATION

▲ Making maps of wildlife and habitats helps conservationists keep informed about animals and their **territories**.

If you care about the future of gorillas and other endangered animals, why not make protecting them your mission? You could do that by planning for a future career in conservation. There are many conservation jobs available. Here is information about just some of them. You can find out about other conservation jobs on page 47 of this book.

WILDLIFE CONSERVATIONIST

Wildlife conservationists work with and care for a variety of wild animals. In this role you would monitor animals to collect data for conservation records that help improve our understanding of wildlife. You might also care for animals directly, ensuring that they are healthy and well. This varied job could take you all over the world. A degree in wildlife management is often required.

MAPPING CONSERVATIONIST

Making maps of animal habitats and how they are changing provides vital information for conservationists. Some skilled geographical conservationists use computers, **drones**, **Global Positioning Systems (GPS),** and **Geographic Information Systems (GIS)** to map species, sites, and habitats. The job is quite varied. For example, in this role, you could produce a map to show the location of a newly discovered species. You could also work through data to map areas where another species is most often found. If you enjoy mapping and computers, this could be the conservation career path for you.

FIELD GUIDE

Field guides are wildlife experts. If you became one you would guide people through natural habitats and educate them about the wildlife living there. You might take people to see wildlife in a vehicle or on foot. Field guides must understand animal behavior and tracking. Many field guides work in ecotourism. In this industry, visitors pay to see wildlife, which helps conserve their habitats.

PUBLIC RELATIONS OFFICER

Public relations officers who work in conservation have the job of raising awareness about issues that affect wild habitats and the animals that live in them. They may work for charities, wildlife organizations, or governments. They run campaigns to make people aware of wildlife issues. They read complicated reports and then explain them to organizations and the public. If you are a good communicator, this could be an ideal job for you. A degree in marketing would be useful for this role.

CONSERVATION PHOTOGRAPHER OR FILMMAKER

Photos and videos of wild animals and the beautiful, threatened places where they live are hugely important to conservation. They can inspire people to care about wildlife and do something to help animals in danger. Wildlife images may feature in magazine or newspaper campaigns. They may also become part of a television series. Wildlife photography and filmmaking are popular and competitive conservation careers. To work in this field, you will need to practice your photography or filmmaking skills to make sure you are highly skilled. You will also need to educate yourself about wildlife and the habitats you photograph or film. Studying photography and film are essential.

◀ Wildlife photographers carefully monitor the behavior of animals, so they can safely photograph them up close.

GLOSSARY

atmosphere the blanket of gases that surround Earth
bamboo a tall tropical grass with hard, hollow stems
boundaries real or imaginary lines that mark the edges of an area
camouflage patterns or colors that help animals blend in with the environment
climate change a shift in the average weather conditions on Earth
communications the sharing of messages or information
conservation protection of the planet
conservationists people who try and protect the planet
continent one of Earth's seven major areas of land
deoxyribonucleic acid (DNA) material that carries all the information about how a living thing will look and function
domestication the process of taming animals
drones unmanned flying vehicles that can capture information about areas over which they travel
encroachments taking over territory
endangered at risk of becoming extinct, or dying out
fertilizer a substance that helps plants grow
fossil fuels fuels formed from the remains of plants and animals that lived long ago
genetics related to the genes and the way in which characteristics are passed from parents to offspring
Geographic Information Systems (GIS) computer systems that analyze and display geographical information
geological related to Earth's structure
Global Positioning Systems (GPS) systems of satellites in space that tell us were something is
habitats places in which plants and animals live
ivory the hard, white material that forms the tusks of elephants
logging cutting down trees
mates animals of the opposite sex to breed with
minerals substances found in rocks, such as gold and silver
mines human-made openings in the ground from which resources such as minerals are taken
montane related to mountains
neglect to fail to care properly for something
ore rock or soil that contains metals
organisms living things such as plants and animals
policy a plan for action followed by a government or a group of people
populations all the people living in certain areas
rain forests thick forests of tall trees found in tropical areas that get a lot of rain
relocate to move to a new area
reproduce to create babies or young
resources things that people use
savanna an area of flat, open grassland, with some scattered trees and bushes
snares traps for catching animals
souvenirs things that are kept to remind people of something, such as a vacation
species a type of plant or animal
subspecies a subdivision of a plant or animal species that shows differences from others of the same species
sustainable can be relied upon for the forseeable future
termites small, pale soft-bodied insects
territories areas of land that animals regard as their own and that they may defend from other animals
traders people who buy and sell goods
tropical related to the tropics. Tropics are hot regions found near the Equator, an imaginary line around the middle of Earth
vaccine a substance that protects animals against infectious diseases

FIND OUT MORE

BOOKS

Bullard, Lisa. *Saving Mountain Gorillas* (Saving Animals). North Star Editions, 2021.

Daly, Ruth. *Bringing Back the Mountain Gorilla* (Animals Back from the Brink). Crabtree Publishing Company, 2019.

Gish, Melissa. *Gorilla* (Spotlight on Nature). Creative Paperbacks, 2020.

WEBSITES

Discover more about careers that help fight climate change at:
www.bestcolleges.com/blog/climate-change-jobs

Discover the ultimate guide to careers in conservation at:
www.conservation-careers.com/15-key-conservation-jobs-ultimate-guide-for-conservation-job-seekers

Hear directly from people working in conservation. Find out what they have to say about a career in conservation at:
www.conservation-careers.com/conservation-jobs-careers-advice/how-to-get-a-job-in-conservation

Learn more about gorilla protection in Africa at:
www.gorillas.org

Discover careers in environmental science at:
https://jobs.environmentalscience.org

Find lots of amazing wildlife careers and what they involve at this useful site:
www.thebalancecareers.com/careers-with-wildlife-125918

Discover what the world's leading wildlife organization, the WWF, is doing to help gorillas and how you can get involved:
www.worldwildlife.org/species/gorilla

Publisher's note to educators and parents:
All the websites featured above have been carefully reviewed to ensure that they are suitable for students. However, many websites change often, and we cannot guarantee that a site's future contents will continue to meet our high standards of educational value. Please be advised that students should be closely monitored whenever they access the Internet.

INDEX

ABOUT THE AUTHOR

Award-winning author Louise Spilsbury, who also writes under the name Louise Kay Stewart, has written more than 250 books for young people on a wide range of exciting subjects. She especially loves writing about animals and learning more about what we can all do to protect amazing species such as the gorilla.